ISBN 978-0-243-41892-3
PIBN 10794051

This book is a reproduction of an important historical work. Forgotten Books uses
state-of-the-art technology to digitally reconstruct the work, preserving the original format
whilst repairing imperfections present in the aged copy. In rare cases, an imperfection in
the original, such as a blemish or missing page, may be replicated in our edition. We do,
however, repair the vast majority of imperfections successfully; any imperfections that
remain are intentionally left to preserve the state of such historical works.

1 MONTH OF
FREE
READING

at

www.ForgottenBooks.com

By purchasing this book you are eligible for one month membership to ForgottenBooks.com, giving you unlimited access to our entire collection of over 700,000 titles via our web site and mobile apps.

To claim your free month visit: www.forgottenbooks.com/free794051

English
Français
Deutsche
Italiano
Español
Português

www.forgottenbooks.com

Mythology Photography **Fiction**
Fishing Christianity **Art** Cooking
Essays Buddhism Freemasonry
Medicine **Biology** Music **Ancient**
Egypt Evolution Carpentry Physics
Dance Geology **Mathematics** Fitness
Shakespeare **Folklore** Yoga Marketing
Confidence Immortality Biographies
Poetry **Psychology** Witchcraft
Electronics Chemistry History **Law**
Accounting **Philosophy** Anthropology
Alchemy Drama Quantum Mechanics
Atheism Sexual Health **Ancient History**
Entrepreneurship Languages Sport
Paleontology Needlework Islam
Metaphysics Investment Archaeology
Parenting Statistics Criminology
Motivational

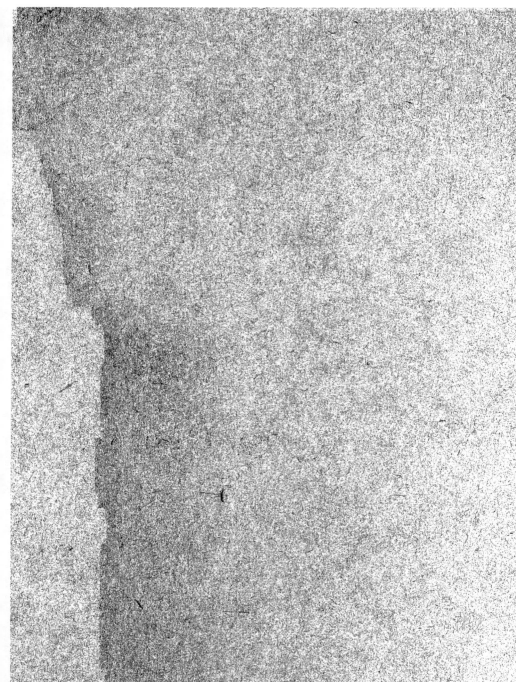

Abraham Lincoln—The Seer

By

EMANUEL HERTZ

AN ADDRESS DELIVERED AT WASHINGTON HEIGHTS CONGREGATION
FEBRUARY 13th, 1925

ABRAHAM LINCOLN — THE SEER

By EMANUEL HERTZ

(An address delivered in honor of the memory of Abraham Lincoln at the Annual Services of the Forum of Washington Heights Congregation in the City of New York on February 13, 1925.)

N commenting upon methods of preparing biographies Lincoln suggested that publishers ought to have blank biographies on their shelves so that heirs might simply purchase such blanks and fill them out at their pleasure with rosy sentences full of high-sounding praise, he little dreamt that he was anticipating what was to happen when his own life story was to be recounted. Numerous are the addresses and papers on Lincoln which are cast in similar mould. His lowly origin and his poverty are ever emphasized; his debates with Douglas are ever referred to but rarely read; his nomination good-naturedly called an accident, and then a casual reference to the Gettysburg Address, the Second Inaugural and his assassination, and we have a Lincoln Day address sprinkled with a few commonplace superlatives, precisely what Lincoln told Herndon after reading that particular life of Burke.

From this method of treatment to that of writing a complete and exhaustive history of the period—1840 to 1865—political, financial and military, and thus including Lincoln, we must at times dissent and hope for a narrative of his own cycle in the history of our country. It appears that foreign observers were more fortunate in their estimate of our great War President. They began to perceive earlier than did we that he moved in an orbit all his own. They concede that no one like him appeared since the days of Luther and Cromwell and William of Orange, not one of whom compares with Lincoln measured by the touchstone of performance. Not one of these had the immense range of mind or the multitudinous activities. Not one of these was called upon to see and speak to so many people in a lifetime as Lincoln saw and spoke to in a few short years. Not one of these was called upon to cope with so many various and difficult problems as was he. Not one of these gave himself so wholeheartedly and completely to a cause as did he. Not one of these had the wide human sympathies which were his, which included love for the stranger, which embraced sympathy for the downtrodden—for the slave. Not one of these with whom he might be compared lived practically his whole life and prepared during his whole life to carry out, without compromise, one overmastering idea, to reach

3

one goal, accomplish one, up to his day unsolvable, insuperable task. And this is just what Lincoln did.

He did not believe in cutting the Gordian knot of the slave power. Europeans saw it first. Goldwin Smith saw and comments upon his first master-stroke which made the South the aggressor. Laugel, the Frenchman, saw the self-sacrifice of the man, how he became impoverished in the service of his country, how he spent the little he had saved and how he insisted on receiving his salary in paper money worth about one-third in gold although Congress would have been happy to authorize payment in gold. Von Holst saw how he, and not Seward nor any other statesman of his day, saw both the problem and the solution. Seward saw the irrepressible conflict but recoiled from the consequences of its solution through civil war, and after a short while in the Cabinet demonstrated his complete unfitness to have coped with it had he been chosen for the task. John Bright appreciated the policy of Lincoln because in saving the Union he was indirectly accomplishing the destruction of the hated institution. It is Edward Caird who tells us that this great American "who was content merely to dig the channels through which the moral life of his countrymen might flow," also teaches that vision and wisdom as well as high motives must lie behind every effective stroke in the continuous labor for human equality. And so on we might continue at great length and cite Castelar, Disraeli, Lyons, Mallet, Montalambert and a host of others, and demonstrate that ours like other Republics, was but slow to appreciate our Heaven-sent benefactor.

Perhaps it was the distance that enabled these men of foreign climes to see the great peaks of Lincoln's Herculean labors. They saw what many of his own countrymen now recognize as the great preliminary conflict fought in the great joint-debates which awakened and aroused the Nation's conscience and epitomized in his remarkable address at Cooper Union—a defiance to slaveholders such as Isaiah hurled at the Babylonian invader from the walls of Jerusalem. They see now what it meant to take hold of the ship of State at a time when half the states were in open rebellion and seven had actually seceded, and in the language of Gladstone were actually establishing a government. They see now that prior to secession Union officials under the very eyes of Buchanan had laid deep plans for dismembering the army and stationing most of it at distant points; for making ineffective what there was of the navy, for stealing the funds, the property, the arsenals, the forts of the Union; army officers and Cabinet officers alike were conspiring to bring about the undoing of the Republic. They see now what manner of man was he who came upon the scene at such a time and dared to announce that right made might. His oath was taken. Under it he had one goal to achieve. All else mattered little. With that end in view he chose his associates and his co-workers. It comes rather late now to perceive his so-called sixth sense. But if ever mortal had it, Lincoln did. He knew what the people wanted, when public opinion was ripe and when they were ready for action. He did not anticipate. He was neither too early nor too late. He was in time. When Crittenden pleaded for compromise, he said: "The time for compromise is gone forever." When Greeley urged, "Emancipate, free the slaves!" Lincoln explained, "We will lose the border States." And when Greeley thundered: "Let them go," Lincoln simply said: "We cannot. The task will then be too great for us to master." And here, as at all times, Lincoln was everlastingly and eternally right and Greeley wrong. But he had to hold the oracle of the New York Tribune, for his editorial page was gospel to Republicans throughout the land—even as he had to hold Beecher, the foremost preacher of his day and generation. And thus he made his decisions. He must have been divinely inspired in his course which was as consistent and as logical and as inexorable as the process of the suns.

* * * * *

The late David Davis, one of Lincoln's most intimate friends, is one of the few of whom it can be said that everything he reported about Lincoln was authentic. "Judge Davis," said Dr. F. C. Igelhart, "the people generally think that you had more to do in securing the nomination of Lincoln for the Presidency the first time than any other one." He said: "It may not be immodest of me to say I did have much to do in bringing about his nomination; but you will be surprised to hear that the first time I ever heard the name of Lincoln used in connection with the Presidency was by the lips of Lincoln himself.

"Lincoln, Leonard Swett, Jesse D. Fell, one or two others and I felt the nomination ought to come to the West. And one day we had a meeting to agree upon a man that we would support. One name after another was mentioned and their strong and weak points considered. At last Lincoln spoke up and said: 'Why don't you run me? I can be nominated; I can be elected, and I can run the government.' We all looked at him and saw that he was not joking. That was the first time I ever knew of his name having been suggested for the office by pen or tongue. The meeting adjourned without any action, but the more we thought of Lincoln's proposition to run himself the better we liked it.

"Lincoln's immortal career began with that little circle and with his own imperial will. We set ourselves to work to lay the wisest possible plans and to execute them with the greatest vigor. Each one, including the prospective candidate, was given his specific task to perform. . . . We put up a desperate fight and won." Dr. Igelhart said: "Judge Davis, I am not sorry you have told me that Lincoln has suggested himself for the Presidency and wrought systematically to secure it. . . . We love him the more we find him so human, that

5

we see that consciousness of power not inconsistent with his natural humility. Besides, I more than suspect that God spoke to him telling him that he desired him to be the leader of the Nation in its time of peril." Mr. Davis answered: "From what I often heard him say he considered himself divinely appointed as a leader in the preservation of the Union."

* * * * *

On the subject of immigration how humane is Lincoln! He said in 1861: "Inasmuch as our country is extensive and new, and the countries of Europe are densely populated, if there are any abroad who desire to make this the land of their adoption, it is not in my heart to throw aught in their way to prevent them from coming to the United States." Yet no one quoted Lincoln when the present law was under discussion. Perhaps that would have been an answer to the oft-repeated question: What would Lincoln do if he were alive today?

* * * * *

A whole book might be written upon Lincoln's services to the navy and we are eternally grateful to that one member of the Cabinet who was content to be Lincoln's Secretary of the Navy—Gideon Welles; and it is from his tireless pen that we get the most trustworthy reports about Lincoln's performances, particularly at Cabinet meetings, which he faithfully recorded on the evening of each day and which he honestly and scrupulously sets down in his invaluable diary.

On March 9, 1862 occurred the great fight between the Merrimac and the Monitor in Hampton Roads which saved New York harbor and every other city on the Atlantic from such destruction as would have meant speedy recognition of the Confederacy in Europe. For the actual defeat, if not destruction, of the Confederate armored battleship, Lincoln was responsible not less than Ericsson. Lincoln had been a flatboatman; he had even made an invention for lifting flatboats over shoals. How few are they who know of Lincoln's patent which enabled him to understand Ericsson so promptly? Cabinet officers, Senators and Congressmen made fun of the proposed turretted cheesebox; but Lincoln saw and understood and told Ericsson to go ahead. With this encouragement the ingenious Swede completed the Monitor and Lincoln himself accepted the strange craft for the Navy. Once more his insight and persistence in the face of ridicule—and he worked in the face of ridicule during an entire lifetime—saved the seas for the Union. I wonder did not Lincoln anticipate all the theories of the importance of sea power in the affairs of men! Again we see that once let Abraham Lincoln make up his mind and forward he went with the certainty that the earth swings through space. This time Lincoln impressed into the service Ericsson the Swede, who built the Monitor; Dahlgren the Swede, who armed her; and Worden the Swede, who commanded her as she sent the Merrimac to her doom and the Confederacy to ultimate defeat.

6

Within a few hours of this momentous battle Secretary Welles describes a Cabinet meeting called by Lincoln on receipt of the news of the first day's disaster. "Mr. Stanton said: 'The Merrimac will change the whole character of the war; she will destroy seriatim every naval vessel. She will lay all the cities on the seaboard under contribution. I shall immediately recall Burnside; Port Royal must be abandoned. I will notify the governors and municipal authorities in the North to take instant measures to protect their harbors. I have no doubt that the monster is at this minute on her way to Washington.' And looking out of the window which commanded a view of the Potomac for many miles, 'Not unlikely we shall have a shell or a cannon ball from one of her guns in the White House before we leave the room!' Mr. Seward, usually buoyant and self-reliant, overwhelmed with the intelligence, listened in responsive sympathy to Stanton and was greatly depressed, as indeed were all the members."

And while Stanton and Seward were wailing about the impending ruin to be wrought by the Merrimac, when Naval experts around Lincoln were helpless and even saw her throwing shells into the White House, Lincoln simply says: "The Almighty will prevent her. This is God's fight. . . . The Monitor should be in Hampton Roads now. She left New York eight days ago. She may be the little stone in the sling of Almighty God that shall smite the Merrimac Phillistine in the forehead."

No other event of the War had created more profound interest in Europe. The rest of the story is familiar. The Merrimac lost all power to alarm the North and for once, unconsciously, Lincoln said outright: "The Monitor was my inspiration."

* * * * *

No two men more clearly summarize the positions of North and South than does Abraham Lincoln that of the North and Alexander H. Stevens that of the South. "We want nothing more," says Lincoln, "than the Constitution gives us; we wish to abolish slavery wherever we have control under the Constitution; we wish to restrict slavery within its present domain, so far as the Constitution permits us to do; we wish to exercise our Constitutional right to prevent the extension of slavery over the territories not yet admitted as States of the Union." That became the sum and substance of the Republican demand; they stood by the Constitution. Well did the Southerners know that any anti-slavery president and Congress, by their power of legislation, by their control of the public patronage, could not only restrict slavery within its present boundaries but could secure its ultimate abolition. The South perfectly comprehended that Lincoln, if elected, might keep within the letter of the Constitution and yet sap the foundation of the whole system. A great and final effort was therefore resolved on by the slave power for the mastery of the Union; and it was insultingly proclaimed that if the North dared to elect Lincoln to the Presidency the South would secede from the Union and enforce secession by an appeal to arms. The North was not intimidated by the threats of the South and Lincoln was elected. From that actual day revolution began. Months before he was sworn in the Southerners, with the connivance or the impotence—some said imbecility—of a weak President, commenced their preparations for revolt.

The first blow was struck by the Southerners at Fort Sumter, although Lincoln was explicit in his every word and act in order not to precipitate the conflagration. The preservation of slavery was the one cause why that blow was struck by South Carolina; and had any doubt on that point existed the statement in March 1862 of Alexander H. Stevens, the South's ablest spokesman, effectually removes it. "The new Constitution (of the Confederacy) has put at rest forever all the agitating questions relating to our peculiar institution—African slavery as it exists among us, the proper status of the negro in our form of civilization. . . . Jefferson, in his forecast, had anticipated this as the 'rock upon which the old Union would split.' He was right. What was conjecture with him is now a realized fact. But whether he fully comprehended the great truth upon which that rock stood and stands may be doubted. The prevailing idea entertained by him and most of the leading statesmen at the time of the formation of the old Constitution was that the enslavement of the African was in violation of the laws of nature; that it was wrong in principle, socially, morally and politically. . . . Those ideas, however, were fundamentally wrong. They rested upon the assumption of the equality of races. This was an error. It was a sandy foundation; and the idea of a government built upon it—when 'the storm came and the wind blew, it fell.' Our new government is founded upon exactly the opposite ideas; its foundations are laid, its cornerstone rests upon the great truth that the negro is not equal to the white man; that slavery subordination to the superior race is his natural and moral condition. This, our new government, is the first in the history of the world based upon this great physical, philosophical and moral truth."

But the question was continuously put, and particularly by Horace Greeley: "Why, when Mr. Lincoln and his government saw that the Southern States were determined to leave the Union, did they not let them go in peace and save the fearful effusion of blood that had to come." Or as Mr. Greeley puts it, "Why not let the erring sisters go in peace?" A genuine American might have replied as a far-visioned Canadian statesman replied; why did not England let the thirteen colonies go in peace? Why did not England let Ireland go? Why did not England let Scotland go? Again and again parts or sections of states desired to secede, sometimes with reason and sometimes without, but whoever heard the central authority of any country patiently acquiescing in the dismemberment of their land?

"Had Lincoln consented to the secession of the Southern States," says this same Canadian—George Brown—"had he admitted that each State could at any moment and on any plea take its departure from the Union, he would simply have given his consent to the complete rupture of the Union and would have brought about a complete failure of the great experiment of self-government on this continent. The Southern States would have gone and the border States would have gone, the Western States might soon have followed, the States on the Pacific would not have been long behind. Petty Republics would have covered the continent; each would have had its standing army and its standing feuds."

"Why not let them go?" Because it would have built up a great slave Republic to the South that no moral influence could have reached. Had the slave States been allowed to secede without a blow all the border States would have gone with them and a large portion of the unadmitted territories of the Union would have been added to the slave domain. Such a Confederacy would have overawed the free Northern States; slave trade would have been at once thrown wide open. If such a Confederacy had been formed with slavery and the slave trade as its cornerstones, no European government would have interfered; and we would have had on this continent under the protection of a regularly organized government the most monstrous outrage on humanity. Had Lincoln passively permitted all this to be done without a blow he would have brought enduring contempt upon his name and the free people of the whole world would have been the first to have reproached him for his monstrous imbecility.

"Why did not Lincoln openly, frankly and from the first declare the overthrow of slavery to be his object in the Civil War? Lincoln was not elected by the whole North but only by a portion of the Northern electors; Lincoln's views on the slave question were not held by the whole North but on the contrary a large portion of the North approved of slavery and denounced Lincoln's policy upon it. Lincoln had a divided North to fight with against a united South; and yet these professing abolitionists would have had him come out with an unnecessary declaration which would have split up his supporters even more and would thus have given the South the uncontrolled mastery of the Union. No, Lincoln knew better. He knew that men would fight for the maintenance of the Union but would not fight for the overthrow of slavery. He desired to get a united North against a united South, and he could only get the North united on the ground of the maintenance of the Union. But well he knew that if the Union was maintained his

9

end would be accomplished. He would then have power to abolish slavery in the District of Columbia, which he did. He would then have power to prevent its entrance into the territories, which he did. He would then have power to induce each State to abolish slavery, which he advocated. He would have the right to put men loving freedom in all public offices in the South, which he did. By these and other means he planned to confine slavery within so narrow a compass that it would of necessity come to an end. By this course, unlike the course of any other living statesman—Seward and Chase, Stanton and Douglas included—he kept his great object in view and prevented open division in the North at the beginning of the struggle. Time did its work; many Democrats in the heat of strife forgot their political antecedents and gradually saw and admitted the necessity of waging war against slavery and thus enabled Lincoln to venture on measures that he would not have dared to breathe at the beginning of the struggle. "I would rather be right than President" did not appeal to Lincoln. He preferred to be both—right and President—so that he could install the right in all the high places contaminated by the slave power.

At this long distance we can see that the South might have fared better had it adopted the policy Goldwin Smith suggests. "Had Jeff. Davis and his colleagues, scrupulously abstaining from anything like violence and insult, put forth a temperate and respectful manifesto, setting forth the proved impracticability of a political union between communities radically different in social structure and appealing to the people of the North for acquiescence in a friendly separation. . . . the Northern people would scarcely have called on the government to go to war. It is here, therefore, that Lincoln first began to manifest his wonderful leadership and his ability as a statesman. While in resolving to despatch supplies to Fort Sumter Lincoln may perhaps be said to have brought on war, he certainly by this act brought forward provocation of firing on Fort Sumter, which precipitated this country into the Civil War with the blame for bringing on the War on the shoulders of the Confederacy and their leaders. He had now swung the pendulum into a position where he was fighting a war to preserve the Union, which was attacked by the South. It was then that the people of the North began to see that the seizure of the property of the United States, the seizure of its forts and arsenals and army posts, were simply preparatory to the war against the Union. It was Lincoln who rent the curtain and showed the South in its true colors. Henceforth Lincoln was the incarnation of the issues of the Civil War and of the Civil War ideas. No man has ever stated the issues of the Civil War more fully, more clearly and more accurately than Mr. Lincoln."

"I am for my own part convinced," says Auguste Laugel, "that on the day when Mr. Lincoln entered the White House he said to himself in the solemn stillness of his conscience: 'I will be the liberator of four millions of slaves. Mine has been the hand chosen to strike the death blow of the servile institution.' And he could not say it aloud from the balcony of the Capitol. If he had done so he must have passed for a fool and a fanatic. Such a declaration would perhaps have provoked a civil war at the North. . . . Mr. Lincoln was like the physician who knows the remedy but may not use it till the supreme crisis had passed."

When he issued the proclamation in September in the hope that someone in the Confederate Cabinet—Benjamin perhaps—might see the force of the document which was to take effect on January 1st next, he finally performed what he had never believed he would have the opportunity to perform. He hit the institution hard whose first acquaintance he made at the auction block in New Orleans. At times he was in doubt as to the future consequences of this great act and this was one of the reasons which swayed him in appointing the successor of Chief Justice Taney to nominate the great arch-enemy of slavery— Salmon Portland Chase. As far as he was concerned the act was irrevocable. "I shall never retract or modify my Emancipation Proclamation and I will never return to slavery a single person who has been made free by its terms or by any Act of Congress." A year after he repeats: "If, by any way or by any means the people ever should lay upon the Executive the obligation of returning to slavery those whom my Proclamation has made free it must choose another, not myself, as the instrument of its will."

The old theory that he was the least important member of his administration has long since faded. While his opponent, Jefferson Davis, scion of one of the best families of the South, graduate of West Point, prominent figure in the war with Mexico, Representative in Congress, United States Senator, Secretary of War, during all of which time he had come to know every professional soldier in the United States and thus was enabled to assign the very best military men to the most important positions, knowing not only his own generals but also the capacity of those opposed to his men, Lincoln had but a negligible military experience of a few weeks in the Black Hawk War and knew practically none of the military profession nor any of those in command of what was left of his decimated army when he reached Washington. How then can we help but believe that Lincoln was as the young man in the days of Elisha whose eyes had been touched that he might see the mountain full of fiery horsemen and chariots of the Lord! How can we help believing that Lincoln, the Seer, saw Grant, Sherman, Sheridan, Thomas and the great army which was ready to spring to arms, to battle for the Republic. If in his agony he saw Bull Run and Chancellorsville, he also saw the glory that was Gettysburg and Appomattox, and in the strength of that vision he was brave to stand alone and assert his will when he thought he was right—Right—his pillar of fire in a long night of slavery's domination.

When by a peculiar coincidence the two sons of Robert E. Lee, one captured while wounded and the other who came to be exchanged for the wounded brother under a flag of truce to Fortress Monroe, were both ordered held until further orders from the Secretary of War, Lee hastened to Richmond for the aid of Jefferson Davis to stay the hanging of his two sons in reprisal for the impending hanging of two Union soldiers. "You need not worry," said Davis, "because Abraham Lincoln will not permit such an outrage." "Stanton will carry out this diabolical purpose," replied General Lee, "and Lincoln will know nothing about it until it has been accomplished and both of my sons are dead."

Jefferson Davis telegraphed to President Lincoln requesting his interference to save the lives of the sons of General Lee and had it sent through the military lines with a request to the Federal Commander to see that the message be delivered to Abraham Lincoln in the White House. "That will cause delay and at least one of my sons can be saved," said Lee. "It will not only cause delay," replied Davis, "but it will save the lives of both your sons for I have great admiration for that rail-splitter President in Washington. Abraham Lincoln is neither a Goth nor a Vandal. When Lincoln knows this case he will save your splendid boys. I believe he will give Stanton a tanning, too."

It was nearing midnight when the Secretary of War entered the White House in response to an unusual mandatory message when President Lincoln handed him the telegram from Jefferson Davis and asked: "What does this mean?" Secretary Stanton stated the case with his habitual earnestness and wound up by saying: "Mr. President, the lives of those two Union captains are as precious to their families as are the lives of those Lee boys to their families. If our men are hanged in Richmond both of the sons of Robert E. Lee should be hanged." The broad humanity of Lincoln could not subscribe to the military logic of his War Secretary. "Stanton, if a crime is committed in Richmond I cannot prevent it, but a crime like that committed under my jurisdiction would stamp upon my heart by command of my conscience the word "murderer.' Stanton, it can't be done! It shan't be done!" . . . Stanton, we are not savages. Let us see what the Book says." Lincoln opened wide the Bible which was always upon his desk and said: "Stanton, here is a command from Almighty God in his Book. Read these words yourself: 'Vengeance is mine; I will repay, said the Lord'." Turning his back upon Stanton Lincoln walked to the desk of an ever-present telegraph operator, wrote a couple of lines with a lead pencil and directed the sending of the telegram to the officer in command at Fortress Monroe ordering "immediately release both of the sons of Robert E. Lee and send them back to their father. A. L."

* * * * *

"During his public career," says Professor Herriott, "Abraham Lincoln wrote some notable letters, justly celebrated for their felicity and force of expression, their acumen and profundity and marvellous effectiveness, but it may be doubted if he ever wrote any letter with greater skill and effect than his letter to Dr. Theodore Canisius:

'Your note asking, in behalf of yourself and other German citizens, whether I am for or against the constitutional provision in regard to naturalized citizens, lately adopted by Massachusetts, and whether I am for or against a fusion of the Republicans and other opposition elements, for the canvass of 1860, is received.

'Massachusetts is a sovereign and independent State; and it is no privilege of mine to scold her for what she does. Still, if from what she has done an inference is sought to be drawn as to what I would do, I may without impropriety speak out. I say, then, that as I understood the Massachusetts provision, I am against its adoption in Illinois, or in any other place, where I have a right to oppose it. Understanding the spirit of our institutions to aim at the *elevation* of men, I am opposed to whatever tends to *degrade* them. I have some little notoriety for commiserating the oppressed condition of the negro; and I should be strangely inconsistent if I should favor any project for curtailing the existing rights of *white men,* even though born in different lands and speaking different languages from myself.

'As to the matter of fusion, I am for it, if it can be had on Republican grounds, and I am not for it on any other terms. A fusion on any other terms would be as foolish as unprincipled.

'It would lose the whole North, while the common enemy would still carry the whole South. The question of *men* is a different one. There are good patriotic men and able statesmen in the South, whom I would cheerfully support if they would now place themselves on Republican ground; but I am against letting down the Republican standard a hair's breadth.

'I have written this hastily, but I believe it answers your question substantially'."

He declares in the most direct, straightforward manner that he was in favor of fusion with any and all elements—there was but one irreducible minimum on which all could stand—antagonism to the extension of slavery. Idealists and realists, liberals and conservatives, could come together on this common ground. The great objective is the defeat of the party in power that favors the evil complained of. It matters little whence come the ballots if thereby opponents are driven from place and power.

The literary art of the letter was perfect; directness and simplicity of language; neither fine writing nor magniloquence and no ponderous platitudes; merely lucid, luminous assertions, strictly confined to the all important issue. Lincoln thus arrayed the Germans as enthusiastic allies on his side by his reference to his well-known views and course respecting slavery, as a solid reason for his opposing any proposal that so much as countenanced the political degradation of any body of white men—and he did all this without giving offense to those who might differ with him.

Just why biographers of Lincoln and historians of the period imme-, diately preceding the Civil War have exhibited little or no appreciation of the strategic significance of this letter, remains a mystery. Nicolay and Hay saw in it merely a statement of his "opposition to the waning fallacy of Know-Nothingism." Neither do Governor Koerner and Carl Schurz attach any significance to it. The former simply mentions it; the latter does not as much as refer to it. We can perhaps explain the latter's silence about Lincoln's surpassing ability at writing letters by the manner in which Lincoln replied to Schurz's unjust criticism when he charged Lincoln with the adverse results of the elections of 1862, which letter in itself is a classic second only to the letter to Horace Greeley's "Appeal of Twenty Millions." —

"I have just received and read your letter of the 20th. The purport of it is, that we lost the late elections, and the administration is failing, because the war is unsuccessful, and that I must not flatter myself that I am not justly to blame for it. I certainly know that if the war fails, the Administration fails, and that I will be blamed for it, whether I deserve it or not. And I ought to be blamed, if I could do better. You think I could do better; therefore you blame me already. I think I could not do better; therefore I blame you for blaming me. I understand you now to be willing to accept the help of men who are not Republicans, provided they have 'heart in it'. Agreed. I want no others. But who is to be the judge of hearts, or of 'hearts in it'? If I must discard my own judgment and take yours, I must also take that of others; and by the time I should reject all I should be advised to reject, I should have none left, Republicans or others—not even yourself. For be assured, my dear sir, there are men who have 'heart in it' that think you are performing your part as poorly as you think I am performing mine."

The letter to Dr. Canisius was of the highest strategic import-ance, and that it must have been intended so, appears from the letter which Lincoln wrote two months later to Schuyler Colfax. This letter to Colfax portrays vividly the troublesome perplexities and the peculiar questions that were then harassing party leaders. Lincoln again demon-strates that he was one of the keenest, shrewdest, most active and far-seeing practical politicians in the Nation.

"My main object . . . . would be to hedge against divis-ions in the Republican ranks generally, and particularly for the contest of 1860. The point of danger is the temptation in different

14

localities to 'platform' for something which will be popular just there, but which, nevertheless, will be a firebrand elsewhere, and especially in a national convention. As instances, the movement against foreigners in Massachusetts; in New Hampshire, to make obedience to the fugitive slave law punishable as a crime; in Ohio, to repeal the fugitive slave law; and squatter sovereignty, in Kansas. In these things there is explosive matter enough to blow up a dozen national conventions, if it gets into them, and what gets very rife outside of conventions is very likely to find its way into them. What is desirable, if possible, is that in every local convocation of Republicans a point should be made to avoid everything which will disturb Republicans elsewhere. Massachusetts Republicans should have looked beyond their noses, and then they could not have failed to see that tilting against foreigners would ruin us in the whole Northwest. New Hampshire and Ohio should forbear tilting against the fugitive slave law in such a way as to utterly overwhelm us in Illinois with the charge of enmity to the Constitution itself. Kansas, in her confidence that she can be saved to freedom on 'Squatter Sovereignty,' ought not to forget that to prevent the spread and nationalization of slavery is a national problem, and must be attended to by the Nation. In a word, in every locality we should look beyond our noses; and at least say nothing on points where it is probable we shall disagree."

Abraham Lincoln's letter to Dr. Canisius exhibited an appreciation of the correlative importance of the fanatical and factional Americans and decadent Know-Nothings who counted for more in the anti-slavery forces than they did in the Democratic Party. The importance of the German votes and the equal importance of the Nativistic votes—constituted the strategic facts that determined the course of events. Lincoln clearly discerned them and future developments again demonstrated his superior foresight and preeminent prudence.

*　*　*　*　*

Historians of Napoleon tell us that he had an uncanny knowledge of detail and was acquainted with every nook and corner of Europe. He knew where to find arms, where to find supplies for his armies in hostile countries; he knew the topography of the entire Continent. Lincoln seemed to have the same uncanny knowledge of the political and military complexion of the whole Union. He knew what was happening in every pivotal State, at every fall election, at every crucial point in the Union; and while waging a great Civil War, while waging even a greater diplomatic battle, while arming, clothing, feeding, financing and supplying the hugest army ever assembled, he still had time for the innumerable tasks of the embattled nation and for ever-recurring political problems. Political leaders came to him from every part of the Union and he had time for all. He was confronted not only by a military map of the Union—the political map as well was ever present and equally important. Whether it was a departing coachman who needed a recommendation, he received it in Lincoln's own handwriting. Whether it

15

was a heartbroken mother trying to save a court-marshalled boy he received her, and when she forgot the location of her son he had time to telegraph to every Commander in the field to locate that missing boy and stay his execution. Is it, then, supererogation on the part of one who never spoke to Lincoln, who never saw Lincoln, who never held communion with those who knew Lincoln, to presume to formulate a theory about the great War President which few authors hardly hinted at, aside from John Morley, who refers to the great emancipator as the seer, as he compared Mazzini's failures with Lincoln's successes? No other author or biographer has made bold to make such a characterization, and yet all that has gone before, all that has been said, could not be the result of chance—of accident. Why was it that this man who had never been a United States Senator or Governor or Cabinet officer or even a Brigadier-General, why was it that this man who, of fifteen Presidents before him, not one but had reached greater official distinction prior to election, why was it that this seemingly less prepared individual by official experience, achieved such immortal results? Lincoln was not even a college graduate or a fairly well-educated man. Lincoln was rough and uncouth. The plain people evidently relished the idea of having a plain man to face the supreme crisis. They had had enough of gentlemen—Taylor, Polk, Filmore, Pierce and Buchanan had palled upon them. The farmers of the country districts, the mechanics of the cities and of the towns, and the young voters made Abraham Lincoln President. And in the very centers of intelligence—the colleges and universities, the vote for Lincoln was almost unanimous. Though it is often stated, and there is much truth in the charge, that our educated classes refuse to take part in politics, yet on this occasion at least they flocked to Lincoln's banner. Some chuckled over his manners, some liked his ideas, some distrusted all opposing candidates, some few actually perceived glimpses of his future greatness, and so this miracle worker grew before their very eyes and an astonished world wondered and began to love this truly humble man. And he grew in stature and in interest until this very day. It is the fortune of but few human beings to become so interesting to others that they desire to know the minutiæ of their ancestors, deeds, ideas and daily lives. Today Abraham Lincoln is one of those few. All the world has asked about his parentage, his education, his struggles, his anecdotes, his deeds, his ideas, his failures, his successes and his virtues. There are more lives of Lincoln, more histories of his time, more addresses, essays and monographs about him and about individual acts or deeds or pronouncements than about any other five Americans together, not forgetting Washington, Hamilton, Jefferson, Franklin and Roosevelt.

Natural historians tells us of a giant cypress tree in Southern Mexico —our Lady of Thule—under whose shade Cortéz and his men sought shelter from the burning sun and under which the Toltec chieftains held their tribal ceremonies. The Spaniards had never seen such a tree in all their travels through the then known world. Its majesty and its grandeur awed this race of sturdy warriors. Travellers pass under the shadow of that tree this very day and it is conceded to be the very noblest type —the King of the forest; for it is as fresh, as invigorating, as awe-inspiring today as it was to the first Spaniards who beheld its majesty. The life of that giant tree depends upon the myriads of roots and tendrils which give it life and sap and strength and sustenance. If we could imagine that tree by some superhuman power completely lifted out, pulled out so to speak, roots and all withdrawn from the ground, unharmed, we could see the myriads of roots both great and small which give it life. If we would study Abraham Lincoln we must study him as we would study the giant tree and take into account every root, large or small, every bit of information, important or unimportant or only half important, which can be amassed and which can be assembled. And so the historian who is to achieve this—another Lord Acton perhaps— and who is to prepare a fair estimate of the life and achievements of Abraham Lincoln must amass and assemble and apportion the work as Lord Acton did—the history of the life and utterances not only of Abraham Lincoln himself, not only his matchless accumulation of public documents, of speeches, and of letters, but all of the utterances of his contemporaries as well, be they those of his predecessors in office, of his Vice-Presidents, of the members of his Cabinet, of the members of the Supreme Court of the United States, of the leaders of the Senate, the spokesmen in the House of Representatives, of the publicists, of the journalists and of the women of the period as well. The lives and biographies of the leaders of public opinion, the books and pamphlets, the speeches delivered at the time and from year to year will have to be taken into consideration. The lives and letters and archives of all the men and women he met and to whom he spoke and to whom he wrote must be thrown into the scale. We must have before us what his generals and his admirals, what his soldiers and sailors thought of him and wrote about him and he to them—of him for whom they cheerfully marched into the shadow of the valley of death. We must read what the educators of the times had to say to their students before they depopulated the classroom for the field of battle; what the teachers of God's Word have contributed to the common treasure of the knowledge of the man whose heart was moved by the falling of a young bird from its nest or by the struggle of a poor beast in the morass of the pit. We must examine what his enemies—and they were legion—thought of him, the statesmen of the South and her splendid soldiers—and nobler fighting men never lived. We must see what the young men of his day, the leaders of the next generation, saw in Father Abraham, and what it was that made them forget home and party and follow him. We must not forget the noble race of War Governors who made every sacrifice

17

to hold up the hands of the weary Titan in Washington from Andrew to Morton, from Curtin to Yates, all these must come forward and tell their story. Their diaries must be opened. No letters must be withheld selfishly for they, like Lincoln, belong to humanity. The memorabilia of the Judges before whom he appeared must be examined in order that we may unfold their experiences with this remarkable lawyer, this honest defender of honest causes. His briefs and legal documents must be re-digested. We must gather the heartbreaking episodes as he passed through the hospitals and as he stopped and sat on bed and cot and stood at the operating table and took a last message of the young soldier of the Blue or of the Gray; as he appeared to his telegraph operators in the War Office, and to the immense crowd of laymen, of foreign diplomats, of travellers and of private soldiers who passed in review before him to and from a thousand battlefields. No one has hitherto appeared who would dedicate his life to such a task and it is the task of a lifetime; but such must be the work, such the task, if the real definitive life of Abraham Lincoln is to be written. And only when all of these indispensable data shall have been gathered and garnered, when all of these have been classified, digested and re-arranged, then and only then will the true form of Abraham Lincoln loom before our view in its true dimensions, in its true proportions. Then we will understand his patience, his faith in the final victory; then we will understand how it is that there was no way to destroy such a man; then we can understand how this patient man could not be turned from his set purposes, how this patience unparalleled, became the source of his tremendous popular strength, and how he inevitably became the unintimidated and unterrified champion and savior of Daniel Webster's indestructible Union.

When this vast material is digested and winnowed we can well understand why at the time of his death so few of his contemporaries perceived his genuine greatness. He had simply overshadowed all and the strain and stress of the conflict was so great that people did not raise their eyes to the heights where he dwelt above the clouds which for the moment obscured their view and did not feel the master hand, the giant grip upon the severed arteries of the Nation.

Charles Francis Adams—like Robert C. Winthrop—one of the most cultured of Lincoln's contemporaries, the very best of the Boston coterie of scholars, of statesmen, publicists and patriots, never to his dying day saw any reason why Lincoln instead of Seward should have been President, any more than his grandfather, John Adams, could ever perceive the greatness of Washington. Neither did John A. Andrew see Lincoln in his true historical dimensions—Andrew, probably the greatest of the War Governors and as noble a soul and as unselfish an ally as can be found among Lincoln's remarkable generation of coadjutors who, after leaving office penniless, without any means of support, declined the most lucrative office offered by Lincoln himself, the one opportunity which came to him to replenish his wasted fortune. "I can accept no such place for such a reason. As Governor of Massachusetts I feel that I have held a sacrificial office and that I have stood between the horns of the altar and sprinkled it with the best blood of this commonwealth—a duty so holy that it would be sacrilege to profane it by any consideration of pecuniary loss or gain." Here was real, genuine, inviting labor for some nineteenth century Boswell! Alas! That task was only partially fulfilled and that grudgingly by Herndon and that only of the period of Lincoln's preparation for the greater tasks for which he had been preparing.

Gideon Welles was the Boswell of but one hundred and sixty-six Cabinet meetings but aside from these Lincoln had no confidants. Lincoln did not reveal himself to any one man. It is only from the glimpses of Lincoln that we get from this vast storehouse of reminiscence, of correspondence, of public statements, of criticism, friendly and hostile, that we can construct a rough outline of the spiritual, the moral giant who held together the two sections of the Continent and preserved what the fathers had builded—and snatched it from wreck and dissolution and oblivion.

The more one reads, the more one compares the opinions of him who thinks him a military genius; of him who admires his administrative qualities; of him who analyzes the sources of his popular strength; of him who studies his early life; his ancestry, his early manhood, his career as a member of the State Legislature, with his short legislative service in Congress; to him who reads the strange story of his courtships and his marriage; who follows him throughout the years of his law practice; the one who studies his utterances, his contest with Douglas, his primitive frontier politics in Illinois, his greatest speeches, his greatest utterances, his candidacies and his elections; the manner of his selection of his great Cabinet; to one who sees him as the good helmsman for the ship of state; to him who sees in him the ever-patient forgiving nature; who used his enemies in order to preserve the Union, who had nothing but goodwill to the diatribes of Wendell Phillips; who could harbor a Stanton and a Chase and Seward—what a triumvirate of discord—in his Cabinet; who could be forgiving to the machinations of a Horatio Seymour, of a Valladingham, even of a Jefferson Davis and a Robert E. Lee—to such a man the fact that he was a seer is the one satisfactory answer to all of the doubts and all of the questionings and that he was a seer seems to be a conclusion as inevitable as was his own method of saving the Union.

We can understand how the seer was at one time abused as no other human being was ever abused or slandered or maligned, as only a seer is, and then we can understand how all the world mourned the death of Lincoln and shed more tears on that fatal day than were ever shed for any one human being in the history of the world: how the great and noble of two worlds bowed in reverent sorrow at his grave; how the afterglow of his setting sun had a benumbing, if not bewildering effect upon his generation; and how there was a transformation of universal sentiment. instantaneous, as by a miracle—the seer was gone —but his vision, a restored Union, remained!

* * * * *

"Is it not Abraham Lincoln?" asks Jane Addams (the daughter of "My dear Double-D'ed Addams," as the martyred President called him), "who has cleared the title to our democracy? He made plain, once for all, that Democratic government, associated as it is, with all the mistakes and shortcomings of the common people, still remains the most valuable contribution America has made to the moral life of the world."

* * * * *

Trees are the most noted longlivers of nature. A tree's age is marked by the bark circles. Every year a new bark grows beyond the old, and in the course of time a cross-section of the tree will show a number of concentric rings. Each ring represents a year's growth. The General Sherman sequoia tree standing in the Sequoia National Park, California, is considered to be the oldest and biggest living tree. This veteran redwood tree is thirty-seven feet in diameter, two hundred and eighty feet in height and about thirty-five hundred years old. It was a vigorous young forest tree while Moses and other historical characters of antiquity were living. During its great life nations appeared, flourished and perished; but the old tree still lives and puts forth new leaves, new branches, new seeds every year.

Still older Sequoia trees have been known. John Muir describes one he had studied in the Sequoia Park that had been destroyed by a gale. It had four thousand rings indicating that it had lived that many years. This tree was alive in California while the Tower of Babel was being built and continued to live as a vigorous and healthy forest giant until the middle of the last century.

Trees appear to be immobile and in a sense eternal. Tacitus, on visiting the Hercynian Forest was awed by the majestic grandeur of the oaks. These splendid trees he thought were contemporary with creation and appeared to be nature's symbols of immortality.

The generations of men who came and flourished on this Continent since the inspired Genoese sailor saw land four hundred years ago and who after completing their appointed tasks have gone to the bourne whence no traveller returns, have produced this one American whose deeds and words and martyrdom will guide generations to come in their never ending struggle for the right, and will stand eternal like those giants of the forests — Abraham Lincoln — America's symbol of immortality.

CPSIA information can be obtained
at www.ICGtesting.com
Printed in the USA
BVHW060921140119
537775BV00010B/2028/P